Women
in Ancient Greece
and Rome

Michael Massey

CAMBRIDGE
UNIVERSITY PRESS

For Stephanie and Jonathan

Published by the Press Syndicate of the University of Cambridge
The Pitt Building, Trumpington Street, Cambridge CB2 1RP
40 West 20th Street, New York, NY 10011–4211, USA
10 Stamford Road, Oakleigh, Melbourne 3166, Australia

First published 1988
Fourth printing 1995

Printed in Great Britain by Scotprint Ltd, Musselburgh, Scotland

British Library cataloguing in publication data
Massey, Michael
  Women in Ancient Greece and Rome.
  1. Women—Greece—Social conditions
  2. Women—Rome—Social conditions
  I. Title
  305.4′2′0928   HQ1134

Library of Congress cataloguing in publication data
  1. Women—Greece—History
  2. Women—Rome—History
  I. Title.
  HQ1134.M25   1988   305.4′0938   87-29972

ISBN 0 521 31807 6

PN

Contents

INTRODUCTION

The study of women in Ancient Greece and Rome is never easy because nearly everything written about women in the ancient world was written by well-educated men of the upper class and nearly always about women from the wealthy middle and upper classes. This means that you must read what the male writers have to say about women very carefully and critically; they are usually describing their attitudes towards women, rather than the women themselves, and what they say may not be true for women of all classes.

The phrase Ancient Greece and Rome covers a very long period of history, from 1500 BC to AD 400. It also covers a very wide geographical area, from Scotland to the Sahara Desert, from Spain to the Middle East. In this book 'Ancient Greece' refers to life in Athens in the fifth century BC because that is the community about which we know most. The lives of women in Sparta are also described because they were not typical of Greek women everywhere. 'Ancient Rome' refers to life in the first century BC and the first century AD.

The quotations from ancient writers come mostly from the periods described above but there are also some from earlier or later times. This is necessary to fill in details which otherwise would not be there. But attitudes and life-styles can and do change considerably over long periods of time; you should, therefore, look carefully at the date of a quotation to see how far it can refer to the periods described above. Your teacher will help you with this. For example, there are quotations from two long epic poems, the *Odyssey* and the *Iliad*, by Homer. They were composed perhaps two or three hundred years before the fifth century BC, but they describe events and people from a period as much as five hundred years before *that*. So why quote them at all? Because they were so well known and often referred to by fifth-century Greeks that they must have had a long and lasting effect on the way people thought about life, including the role of women. And their popularity perhaps indicates that things hadn't changed that much.

GREECE

The status of women

In 431 BC war finally broke out between Athens and Sparta. For over fifty years jealousy and suspicion between the two states (which they called *poleis*) and their allies had been growing. Athens had become the leading *polis* in a group of states which had joined together to protect Greece from invasion by the huge Persian Empire. As a result Sparta had become afraid of the power which Athens now had.

At the end of the first year of the war, the Athenians held a ceremony to honour all those who had been killed. Pericles, a leading politician, was chosen to make a speech in praise of the dead. Instead of a speech only about the glory of the dead soldiers, he went on to talk about the glories of the *polis* they had died for. He praised the citizens for the way they governed the city: Athens, he said, was a model for all the other *poleis* of Greece because of the power of Democracy, a form of government where every freeborn, adult male citizen took a direct part in the running of the *polis*. Near the end of his speech, Pericles had a few words to say to the women of Athens, and especially to the newly widowed wives:

> Perhaps I should say something about the kind of good character we expect from a wife, or rather widow, as some of you now are. Just a few words of advice perhaps: people will think most highly of you if you behave in the best way you can, and if men say as little about you as possible, whether they are praising your good sense or criticising you for not having any.

> *Pericles, The Funeral Speech,*
> quoted in Thucydides II.45.2 (5th cent. BC)

Thucydides, the historian who quotes this speech in full, tells us that he cannot remember every word that Pericles said, but has tried, instead, to record a general impression of the speech. It is probable that the opinion of women quoted here is more what Thucydides *thought* Pericles said or *ought* to have said, rather than what he *actually* said.

Athenian law, like the law of most Greek communities, made very clear the differences between the various groups of women. There were freeborn women and slave women; there were citizen women and metic women (resident non-citizens from another *polis*); there were upper-class women and lower-class women. But whichever group they belonged to, they all had one thing in common: they had no political rights of any kind. At every stage in their lives they were under the control of men.

1

Daughters

Freeborn Greek women began their lives as daughters in a household controlled by a man – the *kyrios*, or head of the household. The *kyrios* was usually their father, although he might have been an uncle if their father was dead. He had the power of life and death over his newly born offspring. If a baby was found to be sickly, deformed or just one too many a mouth to feed, the *kyrios* could expose it, leaving it to die:

> If – and good luck to you – you have a baby and it is male, let it live; but if it is female, expose it.
>
> *Papyrus fragment of a letter from Egypt* (1st cent. AD)

This was a last resort, but it does show something of the attitude towards females at the time.

From a Greek vase showing women weaving.

Sons were expected to work at occupations which would bring profit to the household; daughters were trained by their mothers in domestic skills – cooking, weaving, spinning, running a household – in preparation for the time when they would become wives and mothers in their turn:

> Surely a husband should be pleased if he marries a wife who knows how to take wool and make clothes, and how to share out the spinning work among the female slaves.
>
> *Xenophon, Oeconomicus* (4th cent. BC)

A young girl's early life was spent learning her mother's skills so that she would become a desirable bride for her husband-to-be. In her mid-'teens she was married off by her father in an arranged marriage. Often the bridegroom was a much older man, attracted not only by her youthfulness, but also by the dowry or gift of money that went with her to her new husband:

Of all living, thinking beings, we women are the most unlucky. First of all we have a dowry which must buy a husband to control our bodies; not having a husband is worse. Secondly, there is the important question: is he a good or a bad husband? Women have no easy way out of marriage and cannot say no to their husbands.

Euripides, Medea (5th Cent. BC)

A woman had no say in this matter, or indeed in any matters concerning her at any time in her life. She was regarded as the property of her father and then of her husband until she died. Not getting married was more difficult for women because unmarried women remained under the control of their father, in his household, and were considered to have failed him and thus to have incurred continued expense and dishonour for the family.

Girls never formally came of age, as boys did at eighteen; they were treated as daughters all of their lives. This means that Greek society was *patriarchal* – it was controlled by men and did not allow women political and social rights. It also means that men tended to behave more like fathers towards women – to show *paternalistic* attitudes.

Wives

The portrayal of Greek wedding ceremonies in pottery paintings and in literature shows very clearly how a daughter became a wife. Amid a series of wedding songs and rituals designed to bring the blessings of the gods to the happy couple, the bride was led from the household of her father to the household of her new husband. She passed from the authority of one man into that of another.

A vase-painting showing preparations for a wedding.

The first stage of a marriage was the betrothal. This was arranged by the bride's father who chose a suitable husband for his daughter. The betrothal

3

was witnessed by members of both families, according to law. The amount of the dowry was usually agreed at this time. The dowry was very important in law because whoever possessed it, father or husband, was obliged by law to maintain the woman. If a woman was divorced, the dowry had to be paid back to the head of her household. This meant that women were to some extent protected against casual divorce by a reckless husband.

After the wedding itself, women were expected to live in their husband's house until death or divorce. Athenian women could divorce their husbands and records show that this did sometimes happen, although it seems to have been rare.

> A woman needs to be a magician to cope with such a new way of life, unless she has had some training at home in how to manage the man she now sleeps with. And if she gets it right and her new husband enjoys his life with her, then people might envy her. But if she doesn't, then death would be better for her.
>
> *Euripides, Medea* (5th cent. BC)

Normally a husband expected his wife to be already skilled in domestic tasks, such as weaving, spinning, cooking, cleaning and managing slaves. He himself would train her for the style of life he was used to.

> 'Please tell me, Ischomachus, whether you trained your wife yourself, or whether, when she came to you from her family, she already knew how to look after a husband and a household?'
> 'She could not have known much, Socrates, when I married her. She wasn't even fifteen and had lived a very sheltered life, seeing and hearing very little and asking even less. I would have been happy if she had known just how to weave the wool and how to share out the spinning among the female slaves. In fact, she was very well trained in the art of cooking, too, and that seems to me to be a very important skill, both for men and for women.'
>
> *Xenophon, Oeconomicus* (4th cent. BC)

The central duty of any Greek wife was to become the mother of male heirs. Her husband expected her to produce male babies who would grow up to survive their parents and inherit the family property. A son usually inherited his father's property without any legal procedures. If there was more than one son, they shared the property equally. If there were no legitimate sons, then a daughter could inherit. However, she was required by law to marry the man chosen for her by her father so that he might inherit the property. In some cases she married the nearest male relative who could then claim the property for his own. In every case it was regarded as unsuitable for the woman to own property for herself.

It was important for the head of the household to be sure that any children produced by his wife were genuinely his. For this reason wives were expected to remain faithful to their husbands. If a man suspected that his

4

Mother and child on a vase-painting.

wife was being unfaithful, he could divorce her. The woman was then excluded from public ceremonies, forbidden to wear jewellery, and was regarded by others as a social outcast. This meant that she was unlikely to find another husband.

If wives were expected to remain faithful to their husbands, husbands were not expected to remain faithful to their wives. It was common for men to sleep with their female slaves. They might also seek entertainment in the company of *hetairai* (high-class female companions), if they were wealthy, or of prostitutes if they were not. It was common, too, for middle- and upper-class men to enjoy the company of other males sexually; indeed, such relationships were considered to be not only acceptable but often far more rewarding than relationships with women.

> A man who finds his wife tedious can relieve the boredom by going out with a friend of his own age; but a woman must not let her eyes stray from the only man in her life.
>
> *Euripides, Medea* (5th Cent. BC)

Mothers

Childbirth was a very dangerous undertaking in the ancient world, as it still is in many parts of the modern world. Mothers frequently died while giving birth and many babies did not survive the ordeal. There were no anaesthetics to relieve pain and no effective medicines to protect the health of the mother and her new baby.

> What they say is that we women have a quiet time, staying at home, while they are off fighting in war. They couldn't be more wrong. I would rather stand three times in a battle line than give birth to one child.
>
> *Euripides, Medea* (5th Cent. BC)

5

Women who survived the exhausting labour of giving birth, as many as ten or twelve times, were probably so worn out by the experience that they could not expect to live beyond the age of thirty-five; many died much earlier. Men could expect to live longer than women by as much as ten years or more.

There was a tendency to produce many children, of course, because so many new-born babies died at birth or shortly afterwards. A couple which produced ten children may have seen only four survive.

A mother receiving her baby from a helper.

The mother was responsible for the care and up-bringing of the infants in a family. Babies were usually wrapped in swaddling bandages (quite unnecessarily) to keep arms and legs straight and strong. The mother was also responsible for the education and training of the girls in the family. Girls from upper-class families learned the skills of infant care and housekeeping so that they could direct the slaves in their future husband's household. Lower-class girls needed to use these skills not only in the household but often as a means of earning money for their family.

Apart from the physical trials of childbirth, a mother was also expected to cope with the loss of children and with the everyday trials of caring for their family. But they probably had very little say, for example, in arranged marriages for their daughters, and certainly no control over their sons' education and careers.

Nurses

Mother with her baby in a high-chair.

Most freeborn Greek families employed or bought a nurse to look after the children if they could afford it. Nurses were usually slaves and their duties included the general care of the babies, breastfeeding them where necessary and attending to all of their demands.

> The trouble that baby caused me! Always crying out for something or other. Still, what can they do, babies, wrapped up in nappies? They can't tell you what they want; you just have to guess. Is it hungry or thirsty? Does it just want a pee? They can't control their insides, babies, and many's the time I'd guess wrong and have to clean up the mess! Wet-nurse and washerwoman I was to Orestes.
>
> *Aeschylus, Choephori* (5th Cent. BC)

There is no doubt that the nurse was a much-loved figure for most children and very affectionate portraits of nurses occur throughout Greek literature. Eurycleia in the *Odyssey* had nursed Odysseus as a child and over forty years later is still living with the family, having nursed his son, Telemachus. The nurse in Euripides' play, *Medea*, is full of concern for Medea and for her children to whom she feels very close. And Cilissa, the nurse in the *Oresteia* by Aeschylus, quoted above, has many humorous, yet loving, memories of her young charge, Orestes.

Slaves

There were, of course, many women living in Athens who were not from freeborn families. Many of these were slaves. Some may have been captured in war, but most came from slave-traders who had bought them from pirates and kidnappers. Others may have been abandoned at birth or sold into slavery by desperately poor parents.

Most households bought slaves of both sexes and the slave women were usually made to do the domestic work under the direction of their owner's wife. The younger slave girls were also available for their owner's sexual pleasure, as this extract makes clear.

> One day I had come back from the country and after dinner the child began crying. I told my wife to go and feed it, but she refused because she said that she was glad to see me back after my long absence. At last I got angry and told her to go and see to the child.
>
> 'That's right,' she said, 'so you can be alone with the slave-girl up here! You tried it on with her before, when you got drunk!'
>
> *Lysias, On the Murder of Eratosthenes* (5th Cent. BC)

7

Slaves always had the possibility of buying their freedom by saving up the meagre wages they were paid, but it is likely that more males than females gained their freedom in this way, since their labour was usually better paid. Female slaves probably remained with their owners to be doubly exploited until age and death overtook them.

Public life

Many scholars are still debating how far women were restricted within Greek society. Some believe that most women were forced to live completely within the household, rarely coming out except in the company of their husbands, and certainly excluded from all male-dominated life and business. Others cannot believe that Greek women were so restricted. Women in Greek tragedy, for example, are frequently shown as active and intelligent people with great influence over events. Female characters in the plays are free to move about within their homes and outside. There is even some evidence that women were allowed to attend the festivals at which these plays were performed. It is probably true that women did have clearly defined roles and people expected them to behave in certain fixed and formal ways in public. But there was probably some room for manoeuvre within these restrictions, as the following sections show.

Employment

Not all women were concerned with domestic tasks. Although they did not play a major role in the economic life of the city and were allowed by law to handle only small sums of money, some women *did* work outside the household. The following gravestone inscriptions show some of the occupations undertaken by women in Athens.

Phanostrate, midwife and physician, lies here.	This is the tomb of the immigrant Apollodorus' daughter, Melitta, a nurse	Mania, the grocer, whose shop is near the spring.
(4th Cent. BC)	(4th Cent. BC)	(4th Cent. BC)

The following inscriptions record female slaves who were granted their freedom:

Onesime, sesame seed seller . . . Thraitta, grocer . . . Sanno, an acrobat . . . Demetria, a harpist . . . Habrosyne, perfume seller . . . Rhodia, woolworker . . . Philyra, wet nurse

(4th Cent. BC)

Outside the city, women probably played a large part in the work of farming. Most Greeks gained their living from agriculture and the women must have helped in bringing the produce for sale in the city markets. Their contribution was vital to the success of the farm.

Athenian women fetching water from a public fountain.

Entertainment

Although many Greek men did not approve of women being 'out and about' and working in public, they did, at least, accept that the occupations just described were respectable for the wives of citizens. Some other forms of work, like the entertainment business, were not considered so respectable and were usually restricted to slave girls and foreign-born non-citizen women (Metics). Girls were employed to dance and play musical instruments at all-male drinking parties, where prostitution also flourished. Girls who were especially talented at singing and dancing were often trained as *hetairai*. Greek men saw nothing strange in expecting their wives to be completely 'respectable' and yet attending drinking parties themselves where they enjoyed the company and attentions of other women whose profession it was to entertain them. This kind of attitude shows clearly the 'double standard' of Greek morality – one rule for men and another for women.

Hetairai at a dinner party.

9

Religion

Religion was one area of life where women were allowed to be more directly involved in the life of the community. Women were often appointed as priestesses and many of them enjoyed great honours, as this extract shows:

> . . . the people of Delphi voted to honour Chrysis, daughter of Nicetes, and to give her the god's crown. They also voted to give her the right to consult the oracle of Apollo, safe conduct, freedom from taxation and a front seat at all public contests, the right to own land and a house . . .
>
> *Inscription from Delphi* (2nd Cent. BC)

A religious procession.

Clearly Chrysis, priestess of Athene, from Athens, was considered a very important person in Delphi. At Delphi itself, too, the oracles from the god Apollo were delivered by a priestess.   Other religions and cults attracted women as worshippers. This was perhaps because women had no other means of meeting together or occupying positions of power.

> The women who follow the God Dionysus say farewell to their holy priestess. She was a good woman and deserved this. She led them to the mountains, carrying all the holy objects and instruments. She marched in a procession at the head of the whole city. If a passer-by wants to know who she was, her name was Alcmeonis, daughter of Rhodius; she enjoyed her share of the god's gifts.
>
> *Inscription from Miletus* (3rd Cent. BC)

Many women were attracted to the so-called 'mystery cults' because the rituals and the prayers were secret and could not be divulged to those who were not 'initiates'. In this way women were able to preserve a piece of their lives from the control of men. Men, on the other hand, were often suspicious about the activities at such festivals, even though they had their own mystery cults. In Aristophanes' comedy, *Women at the Thesmophoria*, a relative of the playwright Euripides has dressed up as a woman to spy on the women at their festival and to find out what they are plotting to do to Euripides. He makes a speech in defence of Euripides and in it talks about some of the things he thinks women really get up to:

> Now, between you and me, why have we girls got it in for Euripides? He's only managed to twig one or two of our capers. What about the hundred and one others he hasn't a clue about?'

> *Aristophanes, Women at the Thesmophoria* (5th Cent. BC)

The women are very angry at first when they hear this speech which accuses them of trickery and infidelity against their husbands, but later in the play Aristophanes describes the women's main interests as wine and sex.

Woman at an altar, perhaps burning incense.

It was (and still is) common for men to make fun of women's activities, especially when they knew nothing about them. It was one way for men to try to reduce the importance and influence of women. In the above case it is likely that Aristophanes described the behaviour of the women in this way because he knew it was the way that men would have behaved at such a festival.

Women in Sparta

Most Athenians regarded the Spartans as dull, unintelligent people whose way of life was slow, old-fashioned and unsophisticated. Not surprisingly, Spartan women were seen in a similar light. The Spartans, however, thought that hard physical exercise and a healthy life-style were important. Freeborn Spartans of both sexes took part in intensive physical training: the boys, so that they would become efficient soldiers; the girls, so that they would be healthy mothers who produced strong and healthy children. During early pregnancy Spartan women were encouraged to continue training and to eat and drink as they wished. Other Greek women were expected to have a quiet pregnancy with no exercise or excessive eating. For these reasons Spartan women were often made fun of by other Greeks for their muscular, masculine appearance:

> LYSISTRATA: Greetings, dear Lampito. How's life in Sparta? You look stunning! What a colourful complexion! What strength! I reckon you could strangle a bull!
>
> LAMPITO: You could do the same, you know, with proper training. I have a thorough work-out every day.
>
> LYSISTRATA: And your breasts are fantastic! (*Gives her a poke.*)
>
> LAMPITO: (*Angrily*) Hey! Wait a minute! I'm not some animal ready for sacrifice, you know!

> *Aristophanes, Lysistrata* (5th Cent. BC)

Nevertheless, other Greeks were always intrigued by this unique way of life, where women were trained to be the wives and mothers of soldiers, forbidden to wear any kind of bodily adornment (cosmetics, jewellery, etc.) and did not work at weaving and spinning wool, the most typical of all female tasks in the ancient world.

The following quotations show something of the attitudes held by Spartan women:

> A Spartan woman was burying her son. An old woman approached her and said: 'You poor woman; such bad luck for you.' She replied: 'Good heavens, no. Such good luck! I gave birth to him so that he would die for Sparta and that is just what has happened.'

> An Ionian woman was very proud of her talent for weaving, but her Spartan friend pointed to her well-behaved four sons and said: 'A decent woman should spend her time doing this and then she can be proud of the results.'

> A Spartan woman was up for sale as a slave. She was asked what she knew how to do. She replied: 'To be faithful.'

> *Plutarch, Moralia* (2nd Cent. AD)
> (recording the sayings of Spartan women from the 5th Century BC.)

But remember that these quotations were selected by a male writer and may show what *he* thought were good qualities for a woman to possess.

Image and reality

Homer

Women figure very largely in Greek literature. In the epic poems of Homer, the *Iliad* and the *Odyssey*, there are memorable female characters presented with contrasting images. In the *Iliad*, there is Helen, wife of the Greek king, Menelaos. She was taken to Troy by Paris, some said not unwillingly, and the dispute over her caused the Trojan War. Andromache, wife of the Trojan hero, Hector, is painted by contrast as the faithful, loving wife and mother. In the *Odyssey*, the hero Odysseus is prevented from continuing his journey back from Troy by the enchantress Circe. All the time that Odysseus has been away, some twenty years in all, his wife, Penelope, has remained at home waiting for him to return and has successfully warded off the attentions of a gang of suitors determined to force her hand in marriage. Penelope is shown as a woman of great intelligence and resource. We also learn that a successful suitor would inherit Odysseus' palace and property and would also become king of Ithaca. Some people think that because Homer describes some women as figures of influence and power, there may have been a period in early Greek history when women were regarded as the leaders of society. This is called a *matriarchy*. This idea cannot be proved, however, and many legends show that even in early times women were under the control of the men in their families.

If a Greek boy received any education at all, he learnt to read and recite the poems of Homer. Girls, too, heard these poems, perhaps at festivals or family gatherings. In this way the poems provided very powerful examples of how men and women should behave and what they should think of each other's behaviour. Helen was clearly an example of an unfaithful wife who had brought terrible disasters to Troy, where she had eloped with Paris and who deserved to be punished. Penelope on the other hand was a loyal and faithful wife who waited patiently for her husband to return from Troy. If she seems to be a rather more powerful figure than some other women in the poem, she can still be reminded of her place by her son:

> . . . so go to your quarters now and attend to your own work, the loom and the spindle, and tell the servants to get on with theirs. Talking must be the men's concern, and mine in particular; for I am master in this house.'
>
> *Homer, Odyssey I* (9th Cent. BC?)

Nor could Greek girls entertain any ideas about the easy life that mythical princesses led.

Nausicaa, how did your mother come to have such a lazy daughter as you? Look at the lovely clothing you allow to lie about neglected, although you may soon be married and stand in need of beautiful clothes, not only to wear for yourself, but to provide for your bridegroom's party. It's this kind of thing that gives a girl a good name in the town, besides pleasing her father and her mother. Let us go and do some washing together the first thing in the morning. I offer to go with you and help, so that you can get yourself ready as soon as possible, for you certainly won't remain unmarried for long. Why, every nobleman in the palace wants you for his wife, you, a Phaeacian princess.

Homer, Odyssey VI (9th Cent. BC?)

Because Greek men took in these attitudes as part of their education, they found it natural to regard women as second-class citizens. This story is told about the philosopher, Plato:

Plato always gave thanks to nature, firstly that he was human rather than animal, secondly that he was a man rather than a woman, thirdly that he was a Greek rather than a foreigner, and lastly that he was an Athenian citizen living at the same time as Socrates.

Lactantius (4th Cent. AD)

If intelligent men could think like this, it is not surprising that most Greeks had such a negative view of women.

Drama

The great festivals of drama were important and exciting events for all Athenians, men, women and slaves alike. Greek people attended the productions of tragedies and comedies because they regarded the festivals as religious occasions rather than as entertainment. The huge theatre of Dionysus in Athens could hold as many as fourteen thousand people. This meant that the writers of plays could present their ideas to the majority of the population of the city. Playwrights based their plots on stories from mythology, but many plays referred to events of the day and contained important social, religious and political ideas. The plays certainly reflected the opinions and attitudes of the citizens themselves – who were, of course, men. One woman mentioned frequently in the *Odyssey* is Clytemnestra, the wife of the Greek commander at Troy, Agamemnon. She, with her lover Aegisthus, plotted and carried out the murder of her husband on his return from Troy. In the *Odyssey* she is not shown as the brains behind the operation; that role is taken by Aegisthus. In Aeschylus' trilogy of plays, the *Oresteia*, however, Clytemnestra is depicted as the villain: she plots the murder, she arranges for a system of beacons to tell her when her husband is on his way home, she greets him warmly and welcomes him into the palace, and there she hacks him to death with an axe. Her son, Orestes, returns to Argos to avenge his father's murder and finds himself having to kill his mother in order to do so. Nevertheless, when brought to trial he is acquitted of his mother's murder since it is regarded by the male-dominated society of Athens as more important to avenge one's father than to respect one's mother. Clytemnestra is therefore beaten twice: she is shown as an evil, unfaithful and homicidal wife, the worst kind of example for Greek women to follow; and her murder is then dismissed as less significant than that of her husband. The god, Apollo, defends Orestes at his trial and has this to say about the role of women in parenthood:

> The mother of the child that is called hers is not really its parent. She just nurses the seed that is planted within her by the child's true parent, the male . . . and if you want proof of what I say, here it is: here is Athene, child of Zeus, who was born with no help from a mother's womb; she is living proof that the male can father a child with no help from a female . . .
>
> *Aeschylus, Eumenides* (5th Cent. BC)

Even Athene herself, a goddess, supports Apollo's defence of Orestes. Statements like these from such an important female character, were bound to affect the attitudes of Greek men towards women.

The playwright, Euripides, however, did question the attitudes of his fellow Athenians towards women. Some of his plays present very sympathetic images of women. This book has already quoted from his plays to illustrate what women must have been feeling in response to the power men held over them. In his play, *Medea*, the chorus of Corinthian women has this to say about the troubles and pain of rearing children:

> Those people who have no children have no idea whether it brings brightness or gloom to a family; have no idea of the troubles and grief of being a parent. But those with children always seem to me to be fraught with worry and hard work . . . and even if, after all your effort, your children grow to adulthood, Death can carry them away before their time. What profit is there then in bearing children?
>
> *Euripides, Medea* (5th Cent. BC)

Vase Painting

Nowadays we receive very powerful visual images from the media (television, newspapers, magazines, advertising, films) which often show men and women behaving in fixed ways. Men are frequently shown as strong and active people who get things done. Women, on the other hand, are often shown as passive and dependent except in domestic surroundings where they have to look after men and children. Such images are very common and can influence the way we think women and men ought to behave.

The illustrations in this section show how long-lasting and well-established such images actually are. They are taken from various

A flute-player entertains diners at a party.

types of Greek vases. Vases like these were sometimes used as day-to-day utensils, but others were for ornaments and presents, and the finest were given as prizes in athletic competitions or buried with the dead. In any case, their illustrations were very familiar to all members of the Greek families.

A woman preparing wool for spinning.

16

An amorous scene
from a vase.

Women on Greek pots can usually be divided into two quite distinct
groups. On the one hand were freeborn citizens, wives and daughters: they
are shown carrying out their domestic duties (fetching water, weaving,
spinning, looking after children, etc.). On the other were slaves, ex-slaves
and foreigners: they are shown taking part in various activities connected
with pleasure and entertainment (dancing, singing, playing musical
instruments, making love, etc.). Greek upper-class men would have had no
hesitation in describing the first group as respectable and the second group
as less respectable. The groups are, however, closely linked in one
particular way: all the women shown are, in their various ways, serving
men, either as part of a domestic routine, or as part of a world of pleasure
and entertainment. Men could move freely between these two worlds;
women were, however, confined to one world or the other. The preceding
illustrations show both groups of women involved in a variety of activities.

The public image of freeborn Greek women, then, was one of beauty,
fidelity, chastity, domestic skill, maternal love and affection. Provided they
kept to these and remained, for the most part, anonymous, as Pericles
recommended, then Greek men were clearly satisfied.

ROME

Introduction

People told the following story about Cornelia, a Roman woman of the second century BC:

> An upper-class woman from Campania was staying with Cornelia, mother of the Gracchi brothers. She continually boasted of her jewels which were the most beautiful to be seen at that time. Cornelia kept her talking until her children returned home from their lessons. Then she said to the woman: 'These are *my* jewels.'
>
> *Valerius Maximus* (1st Cent. AD)

It does not matter whether the story is true. What matters is that the Romans repeated the story to show how Roman mothers should think and act. Cornelia was the daughter of a Roman hero, Scipio Africanus, who had defeated Hannibal; she was the wife of a Roman aristocrat, Tiberius Sempronius Gracchus; and she was the mother of the Gracchi brothers, Tiberius and Gaius, who tried to defend the rights of the ordinary Roman people against the Roman aristocracy in the late second century BC. Everybody remembered Cornelia as the ideal of Roman womanhood. When she died, a bronze statue was erected in her honour, with the inscription, 'Cornelia, daughter of Africanus, mother of the Gracchi'. Cornelia may have been famous, but she was famous because of her relationship to the men in her family – as daughter, wife, and mother – not for what she achieved on her own behalf.

In AD 14, the Emperor Augustus, on his deathbed, is reported to have told his wife, Livia: 'Always remember whose wife you have been'. Freeborn Roman women were never allowed to forget that people always regarded them as some man's wife, mother or daughter, and not as individuals in their own right.

Daughters

Roman daughters, like Greek daughters, were always in the custody of the oldest male in their family, the *paterfamilias* (head of the household). In Roman law, the *paterfamilias* had the power of life and death over all members of the family.

There was nothing personal about a daughter's name; it was just the feminine form of her father's name. (Marcus *Tullius* Cicero's daughter was called *Tullia*.) If there was more than one daughter, names like Tullia the Younger, or Tullia the Second were used to prevent confusion.

Letters written on papyrus sheets that have survived from Roman times,

A young woman.

and laws passed by Roman emperors both show us that unwanted children were exposed and left to die in public places, often on rubbish heaps. We do not know how many of these abandoned babies were female. It is tempting to think that more female babies than male babies were exposed in this way since that had been the custom among the Greeks. The Roman evidence, however, sometimes contradicts this idea:

> I sold some land of mine for 500,000 sesterces, although it was worth rather more than that, because I had promised to donate that amount so that freeborn boys and girls might receive financial support.
>
> *Pliny, Letters VII.18* (1st Cent. AD)

Pliny mentions boys and girls separately, which means that many of the children supported by his grant must have been female, otherwise he would not have mentioned the girls at all. Other people also granted large sums of money for the maintenance of children and they, too, specifically mentioned girls. And, of course, a society which favoured one sex of child far more than another would not have lasted very long, since there would have been far too many males and not enough females. We know that Roman society was not like this, any more than ancient Greek society was. Many Romans obviously thought very highly of their daughters, and as this letter also shows, some upper-class girls, at least, received a proper education.

> I am shattered by the news I am sending to you in this letter: the youngest daughter of our friend, Fundanus, has died. We shall never see a brighter or more friendly girl than she was. A very long life, perhaps even immortality, should have been hers. She was hardly thirteen, yet she had the wisdom of an old woman and the maturity of

19

middle age, together with the sweetness and modesty of girlhood. She was very fond of her nurses, her servants and her teachers. She studied hard and enjoyed herself quietly. She was already engaged to a distinguished young man and the wedding day had been decided upon.

Pliny, Letters 5.16 (1st Cent. AD)

The daughter of Fundanus, like girls from the lower classes, was available for marriage at a very early age (by modern Western standards). Most Roman girls could expect marriage from the age of twelve. The next section describes the kind of life awaiting them.

Wives

Upper-class Romans used marriage as a convenient and effective way of making an alliance between two families. It was usually a great advantage in politics because the men from each family could rely on each other's support in elections and debates. Roman women, however, were expected to accept their role and to forge a working relationship with their husbands:

A wife and her husband from Republican Rome.

Tertia Aemilia, the wife of Scipio Africanus and the mother of Cornelia was such a kind and tolerant woman that, although she was well aware that her husband was having an affair with a slave girl, she completely ignored the fact. Indeed, she could not have harboured much of a grudge because, after Scipio's death, she set the slave girl free and allowed her to marry one of her own ex-slaves.

Valerius Maximus 6.7.1–3 (1st Cent. AD)

20

Sometimes such marriages did result in love, but Roman writers most frequently describe love between young men and their girlfriends, or between married men and women who are not their wives, rather than between husbands and wives.

Marriage was also used by the Romans as a means of handing over property and wealth. In some Roman marriages, the girl and any property she owned passed into the complete control of her husband. This was because Roman men believed that women needed the experience and authority of men to look after them and their interests. In reality, this meant that a Roman girl moved from the role of daughter in her father's family to the role of wife-daughter in her husband's family. In this way a Roman husband must have seemed more like a guardian than an equal. When a Roman girl was married, she also had to stop worshipping her own ancestors (an important part of Roman family religion) and begin worshipping the ancestors of her husband's family as though they were her own.

By the beginning of the first century AD, laws were passed freeing women from this kind of guardianship and gradually extending their rights and responsibilities. Women began to make important decisions without consulting their male guardian. The degree of a woman's freedom depended on the number of children she had. The laws of Augustus (emperor from 27 BC to AD 14) stated that a freeborn woman with three children need not have a guardian: men must have thought that a woman who had given birth to three children deserved to be taken seriously! Augustus was keen to encourage the birth rate and was ready to offer this reward to women with larger families.

Marriage was the only legal way of producing freeborn heirs and Roman wives were expected to bear and care for children. Husbands demanded that their wives should be completely faithful and chaste so that they could be absolutely certain that any children were theirs. Wives were also expected to look after the household efficiently and economically. They controlled the family budget and organised the slaves. Within the household, women had considerable power and influence.

> Friend, my words are few; stop and read them. This is the ugly tomb of a beautiful woman. Her parents called her Claudia. She loved her husband with all her heart. She gave birth to two sons, one of whom survived, the other died. Her conversation was pleasant and she moved gracefully. She looked after the house and made the wool. I have finished; be on your way.
>
> *ILS 8043 Rome* (2nd Cent. BC)

Marriage was also a way for a man to increase his social status, not just by making connections with other important, noble families; a wife who behaved with good manners at all times would be acting to her husband's public credit. The Roman writer, Juvenal, composed stinging and bitter

Portrait of a married couple from Pompeii.

satirical poems. In one of them, he wrote a long attack on Roman wives. In particular, he condemns wives whose behaviour undermined the reputation and public image of their husbands:

> Still, better to have a musical wife than a flat-chested, straight-faced woman who dashes boldly about all over town, turning up at all-male gatherings, telling the generals in uniform just what to do – and while her husband's there, too.
>
> *Juvenal, Satires VI 398ff* (1st/2nd Cent. AD)

Head of a woman showing a hairstyle of the 1st century AD.

Mothers

We have already seen how the Romans regarded Cornelia, mother of the Gracchi, as the ideal of motherhood. Some women, however, went to great and dangerous lengths to avoid giving birth:

> Why do you insert things and dig away at your insides, and give poisons to your unborn foetus?
>
> *Ovid, Amores II.xiv.27* (1st Cent. BC)

We do not know how often abortion was carried out in Roman times. It was probably a last resort for women who had become pregnant as a result of a casual affair, rather than as a normal means of controlling the birth rate, as some people believe.

Childbirth was no safer for the Romans than it had been for the Greeks and many women suffered greatly or died during it. Having given birth successfully, women of the middle and upper classes frequently handed over the care and feeding of their infants to wet-nurses. Tacitus, the Roman historian may be criticising this custom, when he describes patterns of infant care among the Germans:

> Every (German) mother breastfeeds her baby and does not hand over the task to slave-girls or wet-nurses.
>
> *Tacitus, Germania 20* (1st Cent. AD)

Roman men clearly thought that mothers were a powerful force in the education of their children. Some writers were keen to praise those who took such a direct interest:

> Every Roman's son, born to a chaste mother, was brought up, not by some wet-nurse hired for the job, but at his mother's breast and on her lap. Everyone praised her for running her household efficiently and devoting herself to her children. Loyally and modestly she not only directed her son's schoolwork, but also controlled his free time and his games.
>
> *Tacitus, Dialogue on Oratory 28* (1st Cent. AD)

Tacitus was imagining an earlier period in Rome's history when he described family life like that. The harsh reality was that many children died in early infancy from disease, malnutrition and the lack of decent medical care. One woman, who was married at eleven and dead herself at twenty-seven, had six children but only one survived her. Such things were not uncommon in the Roman world.

Being a mother was both difficult and dangerous for Roman women. All they could expect from it in the end was public praise from their husband, like that on the tomb inscription of Claudia quoted earlier. This was the ideal of motherhood which women were expected to model themselves and their behaviour on. If a woman did display greater ambition or intelligence, men were likely to regard her with suspicion and to do all that they could to blacken her character.

Lovers, prostitutes and concubines

Roman men, especially those from the wealthier classes, often looked for other ways to enjoy sexual pleasure outside marriage and without the responsibilities of family ties. Roman literature is full of references to love affairs. The women in these affairs were often ex-slaves or women from other parts of the Roman Empire; sometimes they were the frustrated middle- and upper-class wives of men more interested in pursuing their careers than paying attention to their wives.

Sex and magic have always been closely connected and such a relationship might begin with the preparation of a love charm. Although not many women can have seriously believed in this form of magic, nevertheless it was probably an important ritual:

> Bind the three colours in three knots, Amaryllis, bind them and repeat 'I am binding the chains of Venus!'
>   Bring Daphnis home from the town, my spells.
> The same fire hardens the clay and melts the wax. May the fire of my love have the same effect on Daphnis.
>
> *Virgil, Eclogues VIII 77ff* (1st Cent. BC)

In such charms, the number three and repeated phrases always had special magic power, and the goddess of Love, Venus, was always prayed to for help. After the first stages of such an affair, the partners often arranged a go-between, such as a trusted slavegirl, to carry messages between them. This secrecy was designed to protect the reputation of the man, and sometimes of the woman. The same double-standard of sexual morality existed in Rome, just as it had done in Greece, because it was men who set the moral standards. Men from the wealthier classes could visit prostitutes, have extra-marital love affairs and generally enjoy a full and varied sex-life. Women, on the other hand, were expected to remain faithful to their husbands. Those who did take part in sexual activity outside marriage were regarded, both by men and women, as immoral:

> Mind you, if there is anyone who thinks that young men ought not to visit prostitutes, he is certainly narrow-minded (no doubt about it), and completely out of step with our present liberal thinking. In fact, he has nothing in common with the customs and behaviour of previous generations, who were quite broadminded on the subject.
>
> *Cicero, Pro Caelio 48* (1st Cent. BC)

> In the same year (AD 19) the Senate passed very strict decrees attacking female immorality. The granddaughters, daughters and wives of Roman gentlemen were forbidden to participate in prostitution.
>
> *Tacitus, Annals II 85* (1st Cent. AD)

Roman men, like Greek men before them, believed that Roman women were always ready to take part in what Horace, a poet, describes as 'wicked lovemaking':

> The young girl likes to learn Greek dances and, even at this early age, perfects her flirting technique; she plans wicked lovemaking with every nerve in her body.
>
> *Horace, Odes III 6* (1st Cent. BC)

Although older men might have disapproved of the behaviour of young girls, the smart young men of the middle and upper classes had very clear ideas about the skills and talents they expected from their girl-friends:

Chloe from Thrace is the girl of my dreams; she certainly knows how to sing and play the lyre.

Horace, Odes III 9 (1st Cent. BC)

She should know all the latest songs from the theatre, especially those played in the Egyptian style. I think that any cultured woman should know how to hold a plectrum and lyre.

She should know all about those old Greek love poets, like Callimachus, Philetas and Anacreon, and Sappho, too, the sexiest of them all; and the plays of Menander.

And you wouldn't be wide of the mark if you thought that I would insist that women should know how to dance: call for the wine and let her move her arms when she's told.

Ovid, Art of Love 3 319, 329, 349 (1st Cent. BC)

Attitudes like these suggest that girls and women were expected to be of service to upper-class men and to provide them with entertainment.

Dancers from a wall-painting.

It was quite common for freeborn, upper-class Roman men to have sexual relationships with one or more of the female slaves in their households. Wives knew of this and were expected to turn a blind eye to it. Such relationships were regarded as casual and informal. Widowers and bachelors, too, often lived with women. They may have been ex-slaves granted their freedom by grateful masters. Such women were called 'concubines' (bed-sharers). Such relationships were frequently stable and long-lasting, despite the fact that people tended to disapprove of a concubine, although they would never (openly) disapprove of the men. This is a very clear example of the double standard referred to earlier. Some Roman emperors favoured this arrangement and their concubines certainly profited by it. According to Roman historians, however, other Roman emperors were very much the victims of the women in their families.

Imperial wives, mothers and daughters

Roman historians and biographers, like Tacitus and Suetonius, have presented a very vivid and exaggerated picture of the women in the Imperial household. From their writings it would seem that most of the emperors' mothers, wives and daughters were involved in scandal.

Augustus, we are told, was constantly depressed by the activities of both his daughter, Julia, and his granddaughter of the same name. He was keen to encourage his fellow Romans to return to the respectability of family life. He believed that standards had been higher in the generations before his own. While he was publicly trying to improve moral standards, the two Julias were being very open in their sexual activities and having many casual affairs. Augustus finally banished them for their indiscretions.

Claudius (emperor from AD 41–54) is described by Tacitus as a foolish person who had no idea of the extreme behaviour of his third wife, Messalina. She even went so far as to go through a form of marriage with another man while still legally married to the emperor:

> And now Claudius finally found out what was going on in his own household. Having found out, he could not avoid punishing his wife for her outlandish behaviour. . . . It must seem beyond belief, especially in a city where everything that happens is public knowledge, that two people could have felt so safe. But it was absolutely incredible that on a fixed day and in front of witnesses, a man shortly to be consul, and the wife of the emperor should have undergone a formal marriage ceremony.
>
> *Tacitus, Annals XI 26* (1st Cent. AD)

It is impossible to say whether Messalina was just a bored young woman, out of place as the wife of a middle-aged emperor (she was probably fifteen when they married), or whether she was a ruthless, political schemer intent on placing her new 'husband' on the throne of Rome. In any case, Tacitus seems far more interested in presenting her as a grossly immoral woman, and finding a place for her in his gallery of nasty imperial portraits.

Tacitus paints an equally unpleasant picture of Agrippina, Claudius' fourth wife. She was probably responsible for his death, since she was obsessed with placing her son, Nero, on the throne. According to Tacitus, Agrippina is dominating, ambitious and determined to secure power for her

son: the very worst kind of Roman wife and mother. She is shown as the
power behind Nero for the first five years of his reign and when he
eventually arranges for her to be killed, perhaps we are meant to feel that
she has deserved this because of her extreme behaviour:

> Agrippina had anticipated this death for years; she had not been put off
> by the thought of it. She had consulted astrologers about her son and
> they had told her that he would become emperor but that he would put
> his mother to death. She replied: 'He can murder me – as long as he
> becomes emperor!' . . . Burrus suggested that the officers of the
> imperial bodyguard should come to shake him by the hand and
> congratulate him for having escaped from the unexpected threat of his
> mother's wicked deeds.
>
> *Tacitus, Annals XIV 9* (1st Cent. AD)

Religion

Roman religion, like all other aspects of Roman public life, was dominated
by men. The most important religious position in the Roman state was that
of *Pontifex Maximus* or Chief Priest. Like all other religious positions, this
post was held by a person who was largely untrained and who was elected or
appointed to the position for a limited period of time. Roman priests did not
have a 'vocation', as many religious officials do now. People did not turn to
them for religious or spiritual advice. Such priests were state officials, like
officers of the Civil Service.

The Chief Priest's function was to oversee all the religious practices of the
state, to carry out certain sacrifices on behalf of the Roman people, and to
organise and direct state ceremonies.

Women had always been involved in Roman state religion from the
earliest times. One of the oldest religious positions for women was that of
the Vestal Virgin. There were six of them, chosen from the most noble
families to tend the sacred flame of Vesta, Roman goddess of the hearth.
The Romans believed that the flame was the living symbol of the life of
Rome: if it were allowed to go out, then Rome would suffer and collapse.
The girls were made to take an oath of chastity and the penalty for
disobeying the oath was death by being buried alive.

Vestal Virgins were appointed for a period of thirty years – ten years to
learn their duties, ten to carry them out, and ten to instruct others. When
they retired, they could marry and live once again in public. But few chose
to do so, finding readjustment very difficult. They lived in a special house
in the Roman Forum, next to the circular temple of Vesta, secluded from
the public. They went out only at the time of important public ceremonies.
They were treated with the greatest respect. To be chosen for this high office
was the greatest honour that could be given to a young girl and her family.

In spite of this high status, however, the Vestal Virgins were still subject
to the authority of the *Pontifex Maximus*. In this way, their role was very

An ivory carving of
a Roman lady
sacrificing, with
the help of a slave.

similar to that of the *Materfamilias*, who tended the household on behalf of husband and family.

Women could also reach other important positions in the state religion. The following inscriptions show how one such priestess achieved high status. Eumachia was a public priestess in Pompeii in the first century AD. She was the patroness of the guild of fullers (dyers and cleaners), a very influential trade-guild in the city. She inherited a fortune from her father, who ran a brick-making business, and this allowed her to marry into an established Pompeian family.

> Eumachia, daughter of Lucius, public priestess, in her own name and that of her son, Marcus Numistrius Fronto, built with her own funds the porch, covered passage and colonnade, and dedicated them to Concordia Augusta and to Pietas.
>
> *Inscription over the Entrances to the Headquarters of the Guild of Fullers* (1st Cent. AD)

> To Eumachia, daughter of Lucius, public priestess, the fullers dedicated this statue.
>
> *On the Base of Eumachia's Statue* (1st Cent. AD)

> Eumachia, daughter of Lucius, built this for herself and for her household.
>
> *On her Tomb outside the Nucerian Gate* (1st Cent. AD)

Although Eumachia had obviously reached a position of considerable influence and importance, it is significant that she was still identified until the day she died as the daughter of Lucius.

Mystery religions and foreign cults

The Roman state religion was formal and generally dull. It often involved meaningless rituals and offered no spiritual comfort or guidance. Many Romans, looking for something different, turned to the religions of countries in other parts of the Roman Empire, particularly the Eastern provinces (Egypt, Syria, Asia Minor). There they found exciting rituals and stories, and often the promise of reincarnation or salvation after death.

Prevented from being involved in other areas of public life, Roman women were able to express themselves through such religions. The Egyptian goddess, Isis, for example, seemed to represent the power and identity of women:

> You gave women equal power with men
>
> *Prayer to Isis from Oxyrhynchus Papyrus* (2nd Cent. AD)

The cult of Isis allowed women to become priestesses and gave them a status which they did not have in other walks of life. Men were resentful and suspicious of such activities:

> If Isis requires it, she'll even travel to Egypt, bring water from the blistering heat of the Isle of Meroë to sprinkle over the temple of the goddess which stands near the ancient voting areas on the Campus. She believes she has received the call from the goddess herself – as if the gods would spend the night talking to a mind and soul like hers!
>
> *Juvenal, Satires VI* (1st/2nd Cent. AD)

> We all know about the so-called 'secret' rites of the Good Goddess! The flutes, the pipes and the wine really turn on those crazy female followers of the old fertility god and make them whirl around, howling their heads off. They're so mad keen to get into bed with someone! . . . At last they're itching to start, can't wait a moment longer; they're all woman, pure and simple, and they start to shout: 'Now, now! We're ready! Let the men in!'
>
> *Juvenal, Satires VI* (1st/2nd Cent. AD)

Women also managed to reach positions of some importance in the early Christian church, as this letter from Pliny shows:

> Until now, this is how I have dealt with those that come before me charged with being Christians. I ask them directly if they are Christians, and if they confess, I ask them a second and a third time, warning them of the punishment. If they remain firm, I give instructions that they should be taken away to be executed . . . I decided to try to find out the truth (about Christian practices) by torturing two slave-women, whom they call deaconesses.
>
> *Pliny, Letters X 96* (Early 2nd Cent. AD)

Such positions were not, of course, recognised by the Roman authorities, since at this time they did not tolerate Christianity.

Exploitation

It is clear that Roman women were exploited in many different ways, some directly as prostitutes and slave-concubines, others less directly as wives and mothers whose roles restricted their lives considerably. One form of direct exploitation was legacy-hunting. Unscrupulous men, greedy for money and property, befriended elderly, unmarried women, or childless widows, in the hope of being written into the will 'for services rendered'. The trick was to choose women who were at death's door through disease or old age, so that the legacy-hunter would make a quick profit without much effort. Old men without heirs were victims of this racket, too, but it seems women were more likely to fall for the approach of an apparently charming and sincere legacy-hunter.

Actresses, too, were exploited for the entertainment of men, but, because of the double standard of morality, people disapproved of the women, not the men, as this extract from a law shows:

> A senator, or his son, or his grandson, or his great-grandson by his son, or grandson, shall not knowingly or maliciously become engaged to, or marry, a freedwoman, or a woman whose father or mother practises or has practised the profession of an actor.

Julian Law on Adultery (1st Cent. BC)

Some actresses did become very popular with the public and their talents were recognised. However, their low social status meant that upper-class Romans were unwilling to associate with them, and laws like the one above merely reinforced such prejudice.

> In her earlier life she was the star in many towns and cities for her skill in acting in plays, mimes and choruses, and for her dancing, too. But this tenth Muse did not die while acting. To Bassilla, the actress, Heracleides, talented public speaker and biographer, set up this stone. She will receive honour in death as she did in her lifetime, when she died so often in her acting roles. Her fellow-actors say: 'Farewell, Bassilla, we are all mortal.'

Tomb Inscription for an Actress from Aquileia (3rd Cent. AD)

Women were encouraged to develop their skills and talents not for their own sake, but for the sake of men. In fact, women's role in most cultures and societies throughout history has been, and is, to serve men. This may mean bearing children, providing sex, looking after a household, working in the fields or workshops, or, as in the above example, providing entertainment. Because these things have usually been taken care of by women, men have always been free to take part in activities which men regard as the marks of progress in society: politics, warfare, business, technology, cultural pursuits such as art, music, drama, literature – areas of life which even today are still largely male-dominated and male-orientated.

When a Roman woman behaved with more freedom, men were automatically very critical of them:

> Among them was Sempronia, a woman guilty of many misdeeds which showed that she was as bold and as reckless as a man . . . she knew a lot about Greek and Latin literature and more about lyre-playing and dancing than was proper for a respectable woman, not to mention many other talents of a degenerate nature. Modesty and chastity were low on her list of priorities . . . she was of such a passionate nature that she made advances to men more often than they did to her.

Sallust, Catilina 24, 25 (1st Cent. BC)

In this case, Sallust criticises Sempronia, not only because she seems to be immoral (by his standards), but also because she shows the qualities

30

normally associated only with men. Roman men saw such behaviour as a direct threat to their male supremacy.

Like the Greeks before them, Roman men expected their women to be either entirely faithful to them as wives, mothers and daughters, or to be sexually available and for entertainment only like prostitutes, lovers and concubines.

Image and reality

Plautus

In Plautus' comedies, written in the early second century BC, women are all very much 'stock' characters, who appear again and again in different plays. There are nagging wives and cunning brothel owners, and there are beautiful young prostitutes, who turn out in the end to be freeborn girls who were kidnapped and sold into slavery as children. The only characters who seem genuine and believable are the crafty, resourceful *male* slaves who mastermind the plot for the sake of their young, love-sick masters. Roman comedy does not present a very lifelike picture of women, merely a collection of stereotypes, many of which have survived until today: the 'mother-in-law joke' was already a cliché in Plautus' day.

Catullus

In the poetry of Catullus, who was writing in the middle of the first century BC, we are shown the behaviour of women who belonged to the 'smart set'. Some were from upper-class families and associated with the clever, new poets and writers because they found their life-style attractive. Others were wealthy prostitutes who ran literary salons, or clubs, to attract writers and give them an audience. The greatest compliment that Catullus paid to women such as these was to call them *doctae*, which means clever, witty and intelligent. But although Catullus praises their intelligence, such women were expected not to embarrass their male companions. He is scathingly outspoken about women who do not match these ideal qualities:

> What a smart tart! What an amazingly long nose, what ugly feet, what bleary eyes, what podgy fingers, what a slobbery mouth! And what revolting language! You're playboy Formianus' girl-friend, aren't you? And those provincials think you're a real beauty! They even think you're a match for my Lesbia! People these days have no sense, no taste!
>
> *Catullus, Poems 43* (1st Cent. BC)

Many of Catullus' poems chart the stormy love affair which he had with the woman he calls Lesbia. She is thought to have been the wife of a prominent Roman politician who was consul in 61 BC. Her real name was Clodia

Pulchra and she was six years older than Catullus. After a relationship that lasted for three years, she threw Catullus aside for one of his friends, Marcus Caelius, who was even younger. When he abandoned her, Caelius found himself in court facing outlandish charges brought by Clodia. Marcus Tullius Cicero, the famous Roman lawyer and politician, decided to defend him. In his speech to the court, Cicero takes Clodia apart, piece by piece, and with vicious humour. In this way he destroys her credibility and her reputation. The speech is a masterpiece of character assassination:

> The centre of this case, members of the jury, is Clodia, a noble and notorious woman. I shall not say more about her than I must to deny the charges. As a barrister, I must drive back those who lead the attack. And I would do it more violently if I were not ill-disposed towards her 'lover' – sorry, 'brother' – Clodius (I'm always making that mistake!). I'll go easy on her . . . I don't think it is right to lay into a woman (especially one . . . who enjoys a good lay with all and sundry . . .) Suppose a woman, quite unlike Clodia, of course, were available to everyone, who always had her latest boyfriend hanging round, who always provided 'open house' for every man and had an open purse for every young man with a mean father; someone who was a widow without restrictions, living with gay abandon, extravagantly and promiscuously; you would hardly call someone who associated with a woman like that an adulterer, now would you?'

> *Cicero, Pro Caelio 13–16* (1st Cent. BC)

It is not surprising that after the trial of Caelius (he was acquitted), Clodia is not mentioned again and we know nothing more about her. Cicero's mud-slinging tactics were completely successful. Roman men obviously thought that it was dangerous for their political careers to be too closely associated with a woman like Clodia.

Virgil

Towards the end of the first century BC this idea occurs again in the *Aeneid*, the great epic poem by Virgil about the foundation of Rome. In this poem, Virgil created the best known woman in Roman literature – who was, oddly, not a Roman at all. She was Dido, queen of Carthage, a city on the north African coast.

The *Aeneid* describes the adventures of the mythological Trojan hero, Aeneas. He escapes from the destruction of Troy by the Greeks and spends many years wandering the Mediterranean Sea before arriving in Italy. There he founds a new city from which Rome was said to be descended. On his travels, Aeneas and his men land on the North African coast, where they meet Dido, the queen of a newly-formed city called Carthage. She offers them hospitality and soon becomes attracted to Aeneas. However, Dido feels very guilty because she has previously sworn eternal loyalty to her dead husband. She organises a hunting trip to amuse her guests, but when a sudden storm blows up, Dido and Aeneas are forced to take shelter:

> Dido and the Trojan leader made their way to the same cave. The ancient goddess, Earth, and Juno, goddess of marriage, gave the sign; the lightning flashed in the sky to witness the wedding and the woodland spirits wailed on their high mountain peaks. That day was the origin of death and evil. Dido paid no more attention to appearances or gossip, and thought no more of a secret love affair; marriage was her word for it and she used this word to conceal her guilty act.
>
> *Virgil, Aeneid IV 165–72* (1st Cent. BC)

Although Aeneas seems to enjoy the affair at first, he is reminded of his duty by Jupiter: he has a responsibility to his followers, and it is his destiny to found the future Rome. Sadly, he makes plans to leave Carthage and Dido. Dido finds out about his intentions and confronts him with his treachery. Aeneas explains that he had not thought of marriage between them because he has a different destiny to follow. Dido realises that she has made a tragic mistake in assuming that their relationship was more permanent than it was. In desperation, she kills herself as she watches Aeneas' ships setting sail. Aeneas has to watch the smoke rise from her funeral pyre as he sails away.

It is difficult to understand every aspect of this episode in the poem, but Virgil seems to be using the story to show the Romans that they must not be tempted to abandon their country for the sake of a woman, particularly a foreign woman, or allow such a relationship to interfere with the running of the State. Once again, the woman is shown as a temptress who will cause the downfall of the man. Dido is presented as violent, emotional and irrational; she behaves unpredictably and finally destroys herself. The message for Roman women is clear: Dido is everything they must never allow themselves to be. We have already seen the kind of wife and mother Roman men expected.

Virgil was also exploring wider issues in this story. Many who read or listened to the *Aeneid* when it first appeared would have remembered how both Julius Caesar and Mark Antony had become involved with Cleopatra, queen of Egypt, and how they had acted against the interests of the Roman State. Such an audience must have seen something of Cleopatra in Dido.

Women in Art

The images of Roman women which we find in literature are well reflected in Roman art. Sculptures, wall paintings and mosaics all show women in their traditional roles – dutiful daughters, faithful wives, caring mothers, lovers, entertainers and servers of men.

A relief showing
women running a
butcher's shop.

A Roman lady
surrounded by her
maids.

34

Not all images of women, Roman or foreign, were negative. Men were ready to praise what they saw as outstanding character in a woman. One such woman was Fannia, wife of Helvidius Priscus. He had been involved in a plot against the life of Nero (emperor AD 54–68) and was banished by him. He was exiled again during the rule of Vespasian (emperor from AD69–79) but Fannia remained faithful to him throughout his life. Her character is described by one of her friends, the senator, Pliny:

> I am very upset by Fannia's illness. She fell ill while attending Junia, a Vestal Virgin. The fever never leaves her and I am distressed that a truly great woman will be snatched from our sight. She is so virtuous, so truly religious, so respectable, so courageous! Twice she followed her husband into exile, and once was banished herself because of him. She said nothing which might have lessened her danger. How charming and polite she is! What a delightful combination (one not often found) of amiability and respectability! After her death she will be a model for our wives; even we men will have something to learn from her example of courage.
>
> *Pliny, Letters VII 19* (1st Cent. AD)

Such an unblemished character seems almost unreal. Is Pliny really using this description for the purpose he hints at in his last sentence?

ACKNOWLEDGEMENTS

The author and publishers would like to thank the following for permission to reproduce illustrations:

Metropolitan Museum of Art (Fletcher Fund 1931), cover (top) p. 2. National Archaeological Museum, Athens, pp. 3, 16 (bottom). The Trustees of the British Museum, pp. 5, 6, 9 (top). Brian Sparkes, p. 7. Staatliche Antikenssammslung, Munich, pp. 9 (bottom), 16 (top). Alison Frantz, Princeton, N.J., p. 10. American School of Classical Studies at Athens: Agora Excavations, p. 11. Musee Archeologique, Laon (photo Studio Alex), p. 17. Mansell Collection, cover (bottom), pp. 19, 20, 22, 34. Fototeca Unione, at the American Academy in Rome, p. 25. By courtesy of the Board of Trustees of the Victoria and Albert Museum, p. 28.

The text extracts on pp. 13 and 14 are from *Homer: The Odyssey*, translated by E. V. Rieu (Penguin Classics, 1946), copyright © the Estate of E. V. Rieu, 1946, and are reproduced by permission of Penguin Books Ltd.